AF413621

*To all the little ones who have lost their Mommas,
may you find comfort and peace in the words of the Lord:
"Blessed are those who mourn,
for they will be comforted." Matthew 5:4
May this book bring you a sense of love, hope,
and the assurance that you are never alone.
And remember, love always gives. - Melissa*

Copyright 2024 Melissa Casto

Bunny's HeART

Written by Melissa Casto

Illustrated by
Heather Dawn Batchelor

Deep within Whispering Woods lives Bunny,
a kind-hearted, brown rabbit who loves hopping
around the forest with her friends. ..

…but Bunny loves Momma most of all.

Momma would tell Bunny stories under the Whispering Trees about a God who loved them and had given them a very special gift.

One day something happened that would turn Bunny's joyful heart into one filled with sadness.

A storm blew in making it hard to see as Bunny eagerly watched for Momma to return from the woods.

Somehow, Bunny knew Momma
would not return.
This frightened her heart.

Momma's words echoed in her memory,
"Bunny, I have to go get us some food.
Remember, love always gives."

Days turned into weeks. Bunny's heart was sad.
Ollie, the wise old owl, came to care for Bunny.

Ollie looked Bunny in the eyes and said, "I have a gift for you as you start your new journey."

"Thank you, but I'm not sure I want a gift right now" said Bunny.
Ollie hugged her tighter, "Remember, love always gives."

Her heart fluttered just a bit as she opened the gift.
Surprise! It was a colorful art kit with paints, pencils and brushes.
She remembered how her Momma had loved art.

Every morning Bunny took her art kit into the Whispering Woods .

Just like Momma had taught her, Bunny began to whisper to God.
This started to change her heart.

Bunny drew memories of her and Momma and her heart felt peaceful.

Bunny had a friend named Sam who painted with her under the trees.
Sam said to Bunny, "Your Momma
would be proud of the artist you are becoming."

- Ollie flew in closer.
"I see you have been making art and it is helping you."

"How is art helping me?" Bunny wondered.

As she walked home that day,
Bunny whispered to God,
"Thank you for my friends
and the joy art has
brought to my heart."

Bunny decided to show Ollie how much she loved him.
She asked Sam to help her with a special surprise.

Bunny could hardly wait until after dinner
her heart was so eager to give.

Bunny gave Ollie his gift.

As Ollie
pulled out the
painting
he let out
a little gasp,
it was Ollie
and his Momma.

Bunny looked Ollie in the eyes and said,
"This gift of art came straight from my heart."

Bunny finally understood love always gives.

And so it is, Bunny's story goes on…
A never-ending reminder of the gift of God's love
and its power to heal a broken heart.

Meet the Author

Melissa's creative odyssey traverses diverse landscapes within the literary and educational realms. Armed with a pen that weaves magic and words that kindle imagination, she is a dedicated writer, crafting narratives that captivate minds and touch hearts profoundly.

Melissa also founded SurvivingHer, an organization that helps women to change their lives through the transformative power of faith coupled with the arts.

melissacastoauthor.com

Meet the Illustrator

Heather is an Ocala-based gallery and commissioned artist passionate about using art as a therapeutic tool. Her work is beautiful and carries a healing touch that resonates deeply with the heart. She's an art practitioner for Arts in Health Ocala Metro and has made a difference in the lives of many, from teaching art to middle school students to working with Dementia and Alzheimer's patients.

heatherdawnbatchelor.com